You Can't Beat the Beatitudes

GEORGE O. WOOD
& WILLIAM J. KRUTZA

GOSPEL PUBLISHING HOUSE
SPRINGFIELD, MISSOURI

02-0719

Library of Congress Catalog Card Number 78-58721
International Standard Book Number 0-88243-719-4
Printed in the United States of America

All Scripture quotations, unless otherwise indicated, are taken from *The Revised Standard Version*.

Contents

*Dedicated to those seeking to discover
the deepest meanings of the life
Jesus Christ called "blessed"*

1
What Does It Mean to Be "Blessed"?

Early in life most of us dream about what we are going to do "when we grow up." Five-year-old boys, viewing fire trucks in Fourth of July parades, proclaim they want to be the city's future fire fighters. Their 8- or 10-year-old sisters have already chosen careers in nursing.

A few years later these professional choices change. Now the boy wants to be a doctor. His sister wants to be a schoolteacher . . . or just a mommy!

Then comes the desire to be a baseball player or an outstanding National Football League quarterback or running back—another O. J. Simpson! Or, if you've taken your children to a circus, maybe one decides to spend his life as a funny-faced clown or an aerial acrobat. One formerly popular song would urge any adolescent job seeker: "Be a clown, be a clown!"

Adults smile. These "I-want-to-be" fantasies of children are often entertaining. There's a fascination to the creative workings and conscious dreamings of juvenile minds. And it's something we hope they never lose!

But the smiling face becomes more sober as the child grows into young adulthood. And there are still the big questions: What am I going to do? What career should I follow? What job should I take?

We spend years preparing ourselves to answer these questions—specialized training, college education, job counseling—all slanted toward fulfilling our desires for a satisfying, lifelong, money-producing career.

Even our experiences in church have bent our thinking toward such fulfillment. Emphasis has often been placed on being where God wants us to be; doing what God wants us to do.

Then somewhere along the line such words as those of the Beatitudes strike somewhat of a discordant note. The emphasis isn't on what we do or where we do it, but on who we are and who we are becoming. God doesn't seem half as interested in what we do as with who we are. And this drives itself home more forcefully when a person puts it in the first person singular!

Nowhere does this truth come through more clearly than in the Sermon on the Mount (Matthew 5). At the beginning of Jesus' ministry, when He delivered this inaugural address regarding the ethics of the Kingdom, not once did He tell His people what specific occupational tasks lay ahead of them. His whole emphasis was on being . . . on the quality of life . . . on life-style!

During the last years of high school or early in our college or career years, our preoccupation often centers in: Where should I go to college? What courses should I take? What career should I pursue? Whom should I marry? Where should I seek employment? Where should I live? All of these are unknowns, and

8

they occupy so much of our thinking as we try to discern the "unknown will of God."

Without a doubt, God will help us know the answers to these questions, but at the same time Jesus turns our attention to the known will of God rather than the unknown. It is out of obedience to the known will of God that we can proceed into the unknown.

You could conceivably discover yourself in the physical place God wants you to be and maybe even in the occupation He approves for you, and yet misunderstand the will of God and not be truly used by Him, unless you are the *person* God wants you to be.

The very first word of the Beatitudes describes a state of being—"blessed" (Matthew 5:3). Christ uses this word to describe nine states of being; nine descriptions of Christian temperament or Christian attitudes. The word was evidently very much on the Lord's mind and, therefore, very important for us to contemplate and comprehend. What does it mean?

While some recent translators have used "happy" rather than "blessed" in relating the Beatitudes, the original word carries a more significant meaning. This does not mean we should discount the dimension the word *happy* brings to these dynamic principles of Christian living.

The use of the word *happy* conveys the spirit of joy Jesus wants us to enter into. And the quality of life the Beatitudes are capable of producing will result in joy. Happy living shouldn't be the exception; it should be the norm for Christians.

Of course, if we take the narrowest meaning of the word *happy*, which comes from the old English word *hap*, we'll shortchange ourselves. Happy and happiness are related to the word *happened*. Happiness is a happening. It is a spirit of joy produced by involvement in a happening—in an event. Thus, it is based on our reactions to circumstances. It results from reactions to external causes.

By its very nature, happiness cannot be enduring because life's circumstances are never static; they continually change. Some of these changes produce additional happy moments; some don't. Jesus' promise of the "blessed" life, however, embraces both welcomed and unwelcomed circumstances, times of ease and times of hardship, times of health and sickness, times of wealth and poverty, times of joy and sorrow. So we must earnestly press on to understand the meaning of this word *blessed*.

Bless and *blessing* are words common to evangelicals. In fact, they've been so woven into our jargon they've become cliches. And, unfortunately, cliches soon become quite devoid of their original meanings. In prayer, we often ask God to bless almost everything—the sick, the pastor, the building committee, the church picnic, the offering, the president of the country.

Possibly, because of such repeated usage, we think we understand what we mean. But we surely aren't communicating that meaning to those who hear us when we utter such prayers. Far wiser is the person who doesn't leave it to God or his fellow hearers to sort out the meaning he has in mind. If, for instance, when we ask God to "bless the offering" we also spell out the meaning, we might include: Help us to be generous; give us a clear-cut understanding of how the money should be used; let this money help fulfill the purposes we have already agreed on.

We are also familiar with the phrase "God bless

10

you." It has become an evangelical equivalent to "good-bye." So, we really shouldn't criticize comedian Red Skelton's finger twitching as he says, "God bless," or the person standing nearby who proclaims, "God bless you!" when someone sneezes. Of course, the unsaid hopes include: God bring you some good; God make you happy; God give you success; God bring you renewed health.

Then we meet those who get "blessed" at almost every church service they attend, or they talk about how "the Lord's blessing" was on the meeting. It seems to be standard vocabulary in describing a rousing service or an emotional experience. They equate emotional excitement with being "blessed."

Such uses of the word aren't really much different from the meaning of happiness. Whereas one is produced mainly by circumstances, the other is generated by feelings. The "I-got-blessed" feeling is extremely transitory.

Of course, we should not depreciate those moments when God gives us an exaltation in spirit, but at the same time we must recognize the normal Christian life is not a product of feelings but of commitment.

If circumstances and feelings do not adequately convey what Jesus means by the word *blessed*, what does? Sometimes in the Old Testament the word *blessed* speaks of outward prosperity. Genesis 24:1 states: "The Lord had blessed Abraham in all things."

The oft-used benediction of Numbers 6:24-26 suggests that "bless" is related to the keeping protection afforded by God: "The Lord bless you and keep you: The Lord make his face to shine upon you,

11

and be gracious to you: The Lord lift up his countenance upon you, and give you peace."

However, when we look at the New Testament, we see this word *bless* (which occurs over 50 times in its various forms) is never used to refer to external prosperity. It always refers to an inward condition. This fact is vitally important to understanding what God desires for us.

"Then turning to the disciples he said privately, '*Blessed* are the eyes which see what you see!'" (Luke 10:23). "Blessed be the God and Father of our Lord Jesus Christ, who has *blessed* us in Christ with every spiritual *blessing* in the heavenly places" (Ephesians 1:3). "The cup of *blessing* which we *bless,* is it not a participation in the blood of Christ?" (1 Corinthians 10:16). "And I heard a voice from heaven saying, 'Write this: *Blessed* are the dead who die in the Lord henceforth.' '*Blessed* indeed,' says the Spirit, 'that they may rest from their labors, for their deeds follow them!'" (Revelation 14:13).

To be blessed is to receive God's approval on our life; an approval that comes not because we deserve it or because we are perfect, but because He loves us and is gracious to us. This approval of God creates a deep and abiding satisfaction and joy in our life. This joy is fantastically independent of outward circumstances. It is a joy that is always with us—in sorrow, pain, loss, and grief; in youth, middle age, or old age. Nothing can drive this joy away. Everything is powerless to touch it.

God's clear will for your life is that it be "blessed." *Blessed* is the first word of our Lord in His Sermon on the Mount (Matthew 5:3). God has a wonderful attitude toward us. He wants us to live our days continually experiencing innermost satisfaction—a satisfaction that comes because God has approved us. Knowing this, we experience deep joy.

Jesus has a life-style He wants us to enter. Having told us His clear will for our lives is that we be blessed, He proceeds to tell us the conditions through which this blessing is received.

"Blessed are the poor in spirit,
for theirs is the kingdom of heaven" (Matthew 5:3).

2

Personal Poverty
and Its Reward

Many levels of poverty exist in our society. The Department of Health, Education, and Welfare (HEW) has its definition. Anyone or any family earning less than a certain specified income is considered as living "below the poverty level." But one needs to visit only a few Asian nations to discover that people at our poverty level would almost be considered well-to-do in such countries.

An affluent person who has lost much of his affluence would consider himself as living at a poverty level even though he might be better off than those around him. Or a college student might experience what he thinks are poverty conditions when he has to wash his own clothes or forego an extra cheeseburger due to limited cash on hand. To some, poverty may mean a young man taking a girl for a walk instead of to an expensive restaurant.

While these kinds of poverty can be a nuisance, they are not the poverty of complete desperation. Few of us Americans have known such poverty—especially when we can appeal to the government for help. But, throughout the world, many fear poverty because there is nowhere to turn for help, and they face slow starvation or death by malnutrition.

In this kind of poverty a man has no means of support at all. Even his offer to work is turned down. Soon he becomes physically unable to work. And in such poverty, men, women, and children go hungry because there is no food. They grow cold because there are no walls or roof. They go naked because there are no clothes. They are reduced to beggars. And if they are to live at all, the resources must come entirely from outside themselves, from outside their ability to produce. This is destitute, total poverty.

When Jesus talked about being poor in spirit, He was telling us we must recognize ourselves as being in this category spiritually. We must see ourselves, in our innermost beings, as the destitute poor. The destitute poor are under no illusion that they can change anything. All power is in the hands of others. So in Jesus' kingdom, the very first key is realizing only God can get us into His kingdom. As poor in spirit, we must live off the fruit of Another's labor; we must live off the contribution of Jesus Christ.

Paul puts it rather succinctly: "For it is by grace you have been saved, through faith—and this not from yourselves, it is the gift of God" (Ephesians 2:8, *NIV*). We do not possess in ourselves the ability to enter the Kingdom. Our own efforts or righteousness fall short. We must depend totally on the One who controls heaven. We must depend totally on a gracious God who opened the way through Jesus Christ.

The dependent and destitute poor are completely dependent on outside aid if life is to go on. So it is with us. Our spiritual poverty can never be relieved by our own efforts. There is no way for us to be happy or to be deeply satisfied if we try to get by on our own resources. Haughtiness, pride, false self-confidence, and stubbornness all seek to prevent us from realizing our total poverty.

The destitute poor come wanting only mercy . . . only a handout. They come as beggars. They can't come otherwise.

The destitute poor require no emotional giving of self on the part of their benefactor—just physical goods are sufficient. What they need is all they ask for—something to relieve the hunger; something to keep them from starvation.

How differently does God treat His poor! We come to Him for mercy and He gives us love. And He doesn't have to go searching to find that which will fulfill our needs. He doesn't have to go beyond himself. Rather, He gives us himself. Nor does He lessen or deplete any of himself when He supplies our needs. He gives to us out of the richness of His eternal personality. Paul confirms this in Philippians 4:19: "My God will meet all your needs according to his glorious riches in Christ Jesus" *(NIV)*.

Not only does the Christian life begin with the recognition of our personal poverty before God, but it also must be maintained on that basis. Although our souls are headed in a new direction and we can claim to be saved, we are still totally dependent on the mercy and grace of a loving God. It is He who maintains us and not we ourselves. And it will ever remain so. The power of the resurrection that will usher us into the eternal presence of God is the final evidence of our dependence on Him. All power is His and if His Spirit ever withdrew from us, we would be finished!

So what is the blessedness of being poor in spirit? It is the realization that we can do nothing of ourselves, that whatever we have, and especially whatever we are or will become, is dependent on what God does. It is His Spirit at work within us that makes us what we ought to be. It is our spirit recognizing our utter dependence on God. "Blessed are the poor in spirit."

As we will see, and hopefully understand, each of the Beatitudes begins with a character-revealing trait and is followed by a paradoxical statement. The poor in spirit have the Kingdom. Those who mourn are comforted. The meek inherit the earth. The merciful obtain mercy.

How paradoxical! What a contrast in words! The poor in spirit have the kingdom of heaven. The destitute man would be satisfied with a regular diet of plain bread. He'd be satisfied with the skimpiest type of housing—just enough to shelter him from the cold or heat and the rain and wind.

And would not the poor in spirit be satisfied with the meagerest of God's provisions? Just the forgiveness of sins. Wouldn't that be more than sufficient? Or just entrance into heaven without any promise of rewards. That surely is more than anyone deserves!

But Christ says the poor in spirit obtain a kingdom. They obtain an inheritance based on the riches of God. The poor in spirit become heirs. The poor in spirit, dependent totally on the saving grace of Jesus Christ, "have received the spirit of sonship. When we cry, 'Abba! Father!' it is the Spirit himself bearing witness with our spirit that we are children of God, and if children, then heirs, heirs of God and fellow heirs with Christ" (Romans 8:15-17). Eternity belongs to the poor in spirit!

But the poor in spirit not only gain the future, they

also secure the present as well. Theirs *is* the king-dom of heaven. It's a present reality.

The Kingdom is whenever and wherever Jesus Christ reigns as Lord. In this age, the Kingdom is not identifiable by a geographical location. Like seed in the soil and leaven in bread, the Kingdom is in the entire world. Pagans do not see it, yet it is growing. It has no geographical boundaries and no one lan-guage. God reigns now, whenever and wherever men open their lives to receive the rule of Jesus Christ.

The kingdom of God and the kingdom of heaven are synonymous terms—a close study of the Gospel narratives reveals this. The writers used the terms interchangeably.

Jesus Christ exercises complete rule over His kingdom. Other kings may rule over men, systems, and geographical territories, but Jesus reigns within men. He reigns within their natures, making them into new persons altogether. Paul proclaimed: "When someone becomes a Christian he becomes a brand-new person inside. He is not the same any more. A new life has begun!" (2 Corinthians 5:17, *The Living Bible*). Christ takes control of our inner life. Like kings of old, He reigns. He becomes the supreme Ruler. But rather than dominating by force, He recreates us through the gentle persuasion of His love. What other king ever did that kind of reigning? or could reign like Him? None!

Therefore, when Jesus says the poor in spirit have the Kingdom now, He is telling us that even today we will see the power of His reigning breaking through into our lives. He has the power to defeat our enemy, Satan. As Matthew says, Christ enters the strong man's house, binds him, and plunders his

19

goods (Matthew 12:29). In other words, through the life and passion of Jesus, He has manifested His victory over Satan. Today Christ is at work taking men out of the devil's clutches. He is setting up His kingdom in the hearts of men. We possess His kingdom now as it is operative within us. And in possessing the kingdom of God, we not only experience the force of Jesus' words as King (His teachings), but also His mighty power as well. The power of God continually operates in our lives, transforming us to better represent the King.

At the close of His ministry, Jesus told His disciples: "All power in Heaven and on earth has been given to me" (Matthew 28:18, *Phillips*). Jesus does not have just some power or a little power, He has *all* power! The disciples could not make disciples, baptize, teach, and heal unless they understood their utter inability and powerlessness while standing alongside the powerful Christ. They simply needed to draw from His power. All authority and power are resident in Him. And the same is true for us today!

It's so important that we realize this. God sets His approval on us, which results in our being deeply joyful, as we become poor in spirit before Him. There is no room for a big head in the kingdom of God. We are to take the mind of a servant, even as Christ chose to do. We are to honor one another, preferring one another above ourselves (Romans 12:10).

It is the poverty of our own resources that drives us to dependence on God. Our acknowledged nothingness before God makes room for the power of Christ's kingdom to manifest itself in and through us.

God's will today is: "Blessed are the poor in spirit, for theirs is the kingdom of heaven."

*"Blessed are those who mourn,
for they shall be comforted"* (Matthew 5:4).

3

Grief That Leads to Comfort

Jesus says His people are to be blessed. Happy! Then why aren't they laughing? Where has all the happiness gone? Didn't God create us with the unique ability to see the incongruities of life—and laugh? Or doesn't God supply us with the inner fiber of character that produces a continuous flow of joy? Isn't joy one of the fruit of the Spirit's work in our lives that eventually gets to the surface—and produces a smile?

But when Jesus talked about the "blessed" life, He took an entirely different approach. And if we'd scrutinize His approach, we'd discover little public-relations value in the concept He presented: "Blessed are those who mourn." To attract others, we've been led to believe we need to maintain a smiling-faced witness. We've been taught to pull a curtain over our inner struggles. Don't let the outside world know everything happening inside you. In case things aren't rosy, maintain a stiff upper lip. Freeze your face into a constant smile and sing, "I've got the joy, joy, joy, down in my heart," even though it may be so deep within it would take a special angelic

21

search party to discover its presence. For how will the world ever be saved if we don't present the image of happiness and tranquility—a life in which troubles don't exist? A life in which they too will soon wear the religious smile—plastic grin though it be!

In His statement, "Blessed are those who mourn," Jesus shows no interest in public-relations gimmicks. He isn't interested in presenting an escape from reality. He brushes aside all our efforts to make quick converts to a happy life. He desires an attitude of life that is genuine and authentic before God and others.

In reality, it is the honest, intense encounter with God that truly attracts others to Christ. Any false gloss of our deepest emotional experiences only cheats the seeker.

It cannot be supposed that in this passage Jesus is placing a blessing on all those to whom tragedy comes. This Beatitude doesn't register God's automatic approval on all those who weep because of death, sickness, misfortune, or calamity.

How superficial, and almost heartless, are some of the remarks some Christians make when others face heartbreaking experiences. We've all heard them. The pious religionist who quotes Romans 8:28, "We know that in everything God works for good with those who love him, who are called according to his purpose," when visiting the spouse of a loved one who has just died. Or the one who tells the weeping parents whose child is dead that God will bless them in their tears and, "It was a blessing God took him because he suffered so much."

Such comfort often infers that God would not have blessed the parents if they hadn't been filled with sorrow. But they would humanly grieve with or without God's blessing. All humans have the capacity to grieve, inwardly or outwardly, when a loved one dies or is injured. Whenever human attachments are severed, people express sorrow. But a blessing on all those who weep because of tragedy isn't automatic. Multitudes of those who sorrow have no contact with God. Many refuse the very comfort Jesus promised to provide—deliverance from sin and death.

Nor did Jesus have in mind in this verse the often mistaken idea that sickness, misfortune, calamity, and financial reverses somehow automatically produce an enrichment of human character. Although many can testify that during such experiences they were drawn Christward, this is not an automatic result. People in similar situations turn bitter or learn nothing from the sorrows of life. Others simply endure until the negative experience is over.

It must be understood that Jesus did not present this Beatitude as a condemnation on laughter. Surely the God who created us with this unique quality will allow us ample opportunity for the fullest expression of it. We are only beginning to understand the therapeutic value of laughter—something we can be sure God knew right from the beginning. But as Solomon understood, there is "a time to weep, and a time to laugh; a time to mourn, and a time to dance" (Ecclesiastes 3:4).

In Luke's abbreviated presentation of the Beatitudes, he states that Jesus said, "Blessed are you that weep now, for you shall laugh." And conversely, "Woe to you that laugh now, for you shall mourn and weep" (Luke 6:21, 25). Jesus fully understood the sayings of Solomon!

In the first Beatitude when Jesus placed a blessing on the poor in spirit, He wasn't talking about the poor who can make it on their own. He was referring to the destitute poor—those who need to depend utterly on God. Then He turned to the natural outcome of the person who is so destitute he knows in himself he can't make it. Does not that person mourn? Isn't there an anguish that finds no solace?

How would you express the emotion of a father who is totally unable to feed, clothe, and house his bedraggled wife and family? How can you express the pathos of the person who just cannot make it on his own . . . and knows he never will? What else can he do but weep? His condition leads to sorrow in its most intense forms and most anguishing expressions. It is then we can apply the understanding and fulfilling words of Jesus, "Blessed are those who mourn."

When Jesus talks to us about being in His kingdom, He uses words of ultimate meaning. Only the totally destitute poor get into His kingdom. They recognize that entrance can only be accomplished by the work of God. Their entrance into the Kingdom involves much more than a cold transaction—such as a financial transaction at a bank. Entrance into His kingdom must come by an experience like that of the prodigal son, who not only recognized his poverty but also followed that recognition with repentance: "Father, I have sinned against heaven and before you; I am no longer worthy to be called your son" (Luke 15:18, 19).

As our poverty is spoken of in terms of ultimate destitution, so the word Jesus selects—*mourn*—describes a grief too deep to be concealed. One's repentance and sorrow for sin, for coming short of the

Kingdom, is so great the effect of that repentance is clearly visible to God, to others, and to ourselves. "Blessed are those who mourn!" There's absolutely no need to hide our grief over our sinful natures or our repentance.

What Jesus is saying in these first two Beatitudes is that only those who are willing to forsake false pride, to humble themselves and become destitute—totally dependent on God's resources—get into His kingdom. This act of destitution necessarily is accompanied by a heart attitude that completely grieves over one's sins and shortcomings. It's far more than reciting the well-known truths of Romans 3:10-12: "None is righteous, no, not one; no one understands, no one seeks for God. All have turned aside, together they have gone wrong; no one does good, not even one." It's more than intellectual acceptance of doctrinal facts. It's willful acknowledgment of being personally offensive to God—and openly acknowledging that offense.

These individual acts of destitution and mourning are opposite to the spirit of the world. What, for example, do television entertainers know about destitution and brokenness before God? They may sometimes discuss ideas about God, but show no inclination to obey His commandments. If there is grief in their own lives, they conceal it with a flippant attitude, immoral innuendos, and laughs that tease but never arise out of the depths of the heart.

Is this what happiness is? To act like the world isn't coming to an end? To pretend the day of death will never come? that death might happen to others, but never to us? And to never think about what is beyond the grave? Surely the world acts as if Jesus Christ makes no difference; that He never rose from

25

the dead. They simply go on living and laughing in the television-type vacuum of this world; never humbling themselves before an almighty, holy God. They attempt to be witty and go on in arrogance, never yielding to the conviction the Holy Spirit brings to the human conscience. But someday they will hear the words of Jesus: "Woe to you that laugh now, for you shall . . . weep." And great will be the tears thereof!

All their foolhardiness, silliness, playing on words, high and mighty pride, snobbery, concern with themselves, joking, and immoral conversation will come under the blow of Christ's mighty words: "Woe to you that laugh. . . ."

But then come His unbeatable words: "Blessed are those who mourn." How can this be? How can we weep to be happy? Isn't this a contradiction? Or is it a divinely conceived principle?

What if you let a number of days or even weeks go by without taking a bath? Finally, the moment for cleansing presents itself. How different is this bath from the daily quickies or showerings! After going for weeks without soap and water, more than one quick swipe of the washcloth is needed. You must begin to scrub or even use pumice. If you are extensively caked with dirt, it may even be necessary to soak for a while and then take a stiff brush to attack especially dirty spots. Such vigorous activity hurts the skin that lies beneath all the grime. But the rubbing and brushing are necessary if you are to come clean!

What happens when you go endless days without the confession of sin and prayer? Your soul collects dirt. Let that dirt remain without daily washing with the Word and by the Spirit, and your soul becomes quite crusted. When you finally yield to the Spirit, you'll find you'll weep and even break as never before. Why? You'll sense yourself as dirty before God. Your sins will rise as a stench before Him. You'll sense your offensive condition. As you allow the Spirit to bathe you, you'll realize His power to cleanse you thoroughly. In the process, He might have to rub the sin quite vigorously. It isn't all on the surface. You've let it penetrate deep into your personality. His activity will hurt, but it will also produce healing. Do not deny yourself the most blessed experience of weeping—inwardly and/or outwardly—in the presence of God as He does His job of thorough cleansing.

How beautiful the results of the soul's cry, "Purge me with hyssop, and I shall be clean; wash me, and I shall be whiter than snow" (Psalm 51:7).

The separation we have caused between ourselves and God ends in reconciliation. And it's natural for the tears to come . . . then the divinely given happiness!

The Christian's whole life-style should be characterized by an honest attitude of brokenness before God. And although the tears may come, the emphasis is not necessarily on the presence of tears or on crying whenever you speak. That can become as false as the everlasting smiles of television entertainers. True brokenness need rarely show itself in public display. It is a condition of the heart best expressed in private contacts with the Lord. It is then that one is assured of God's approval on mourning.

Jesus further shows us that this attitude of brokenness not only applies to our relationship to God, but also to others. The whole Christian life must be lived in sensitivity toward others and the realization that

27

we are no better than they. We must care for the suffering, the disadvantaged, the orphans and widows, and those without God. We must care so much that we intercede with our prayers, we help with our money—and, yes, we even serve with our lives.

In Matthew 23 we read of Jesus' denunciation of the Pharisees. He did so without glee or self-satisfaction. While hitting the opposition, He pulled no punches and even threatened them with hell. We leap forward to approve this damnation of religious hypocrisy and would even have told Jesus to put the knife into this religious group. Prick them more, Lord!

Just then we look into His eyes and notice that all the while He has been speaking these harsh words, He has been inwardly crying. It comes out at the end when, from a broken heart, He utters:

O Jerusalem, Jerusalem, killing the prophets and stoning those who are sent to you! How often would I have gathered your children together as a hen gathers her brood under her wings, and you would not! (Matthew 23:37).

Jesus wept over the lostness of a city filled with people who would soon cry out for Roman soldiers to lead Him away to a hill called Calvary, where on a cruel cross they would crucify Him between two thieves. What dimension the truth of His compassion gives to the Christian community. We cannot hate the people, or even one individual, over whose actions our soul is deeply grieved.

It is not enough to say, "I'll let someone else take the lead in this mourning bit, and when I'm convinced it's genuine, I'll join in." Such following the leader would be hypocrisy. Each of us is responsible for his own soul before God. To learn the secret of honest mourning is to have the compassionate attitude of Christ penetrate our personality. Truly it can only be the work of the Holy Spirit within. All other mourning is as false as that demonstrated by the paid weepers at a Jewish funeral.

"Blessed are those who mourn." Jesus announces that God approves the man or woman who grieves over his own spiritual destitution. But His blessing not only includes the promise of God's approval, it also results in an inward condition: "They shall be comforted."

The word Jesus uses for comfort carries more than the promise of a pat on the shoulder. It means far more than a duplication of our feeble attempts to alleviate the inward pains of those who have recently experienced sorrow-bringing events. It means God actually comes to our aid and changes the situation over which we have been grieving. It means the coming of God as Comforter, even as Jesus promised in John 14:16. Those who have gone through the experience of mourning before God sense His divine presence in forgiveness and acceptance. And what greater comfort than to experience acceptance by a compassionate, loving Lord?

God blesses the repentant heart by completely eradicating the irremovable scarlet dye of sin. God's comfort comes as He changes our sinful condition. Forgiveness follows confession. Harmony follows rancor. Reconciliation replaces bitterness. Deep joy follows sorrow.

With the Psalmist, the mournful who have received God's comfort, can declare:

Sing praises to the Lord, O you his saints, and give thanks to his holy name. For his anger is but for a moment, and his favor is for a lifetime. Weeping may tarry for the night, but joy comes with the morning (Psalm 30:4, 5).

Have you experienced the blessedness of this second Beatitude? Nothing can outdo it in making the comfort of God a viable force within and a visible testimony without.

"Blessed are those who mourn, for they shall be comforted." If you have experienced the first in your private contacts with your God, you're surely in line for the second!

"Blessed are the meek,
for they shall inherit the earth" (Matthew 5:5).

4

Not Given to Extremes

Whether we want to admit it or not, people usually have names they call us when we are not around. Or at least they identify us by certain characteristics—either negative or positive, whichever seem to impress them the most. We feel good, therefore, when we accidently hear someone's positive evaluation of us: "He's sharp!" "He's handsome!" "She's a charming person." "She's great to be around."

Conversely, we are unhappy when we overhear negative remarks: "He's a bore." "He thinks he knows it all." "What a pain!" "She's a witch!" There's something within every one of us that cringes at negative evaluations. We'd wish others would see us more like we'd like to be seen, or more like we evaluate ourselves.

Then there are those in-between terms used to describe us at various times when it seems the observer wishes to remain neutral. Many people have developed and use a variety of safe cliches, for example: "He's okay." "She's nice."

We're not sure whether we'd ever want someone to evaluate us as "meek." Meek is one of those words

31

that gets a negative response from most of us or, at best, rates about even with "okay" and "nice." Who wants to go around, or even survive, in this big bad world with this epithet strung around his neck: "He's meek"? What young fellow would like this as a Saturday night, after-dating evaluation by the girls in the college dorm: "He's a meek fellow"? What salesman would appreciate this evaluation from his sales manager: "You're a meek man, Jones"? What young woman would appreciate the personnel manager's "meek" listing at the top of her application after an interview for a position dealing with the public?

The word *meek*, for many men, connotes being a sissy, being more effeminate than male, being timid and afraid of oneself and of others, and being fearful of asserting oneself lest others be offended. Almost everyone who considers himself an adequate, fully matured person shies away from such a designation. It is therefore understandable why some have tagged Christianity with a sissy image when they've heard this oft-recited Beatitude: "Blessed are the meek."

Those giving such an evaluation of Christianity think Christ wants men who are more effeminate than brawny. Or they picture Jesus as a kind, gentle, rather milk-toast visionary who was afraid to step on a wiggly caterpillar and who never seemed to get His head completely out of the clouds. So it comes as no surprise that Jesus has sometimes been painted as a pale, skinny Galilean whose greatest appeal is to men who are less than totally developed in body and mind, and to women of like ilk.

Before you forever settle in your mind that Jesus had these ideas of meekness, at least consider this:

Did Jesus ever ask His men to be something He himself was not?

Along with this, you need to answer a few other questions:

Was Jesus a Man with a weak will or a strong one?

Was Jesus gainfully employed as a carpenter (in the days before there were power tools or even steel blades) or as a manicurist?

Did Jesus ever get anyone violently angry with Him or did He just try to smooth over people's ruffled feelings?

Did Jesus ever show any strong emotions—like being angry—or did He go through life placidly with never a ripple of feeling?

Laying aside the fact that He was divine, is there much in Jesus the Man that you can respect or admire or even adapt to your own life?

You know the answers to all these questions!

During His growing-up years, Jesus worked as a carpenter's apprentice. He probably swung an axe quite frequently to hew timbers into usable lumber. Or He drove large wooden pegs with a crude sledge hammer. Physically, He was most likely tough as nails; possibly one of the tougher youths in the city of Nazareth.

After He began His ministry, people readily recognized Him but asked one another to make sure, "Is not this the carpenter's son?" (Matthew 13:55). Besides, He had a will to match His physical prowess. Jesus evidenced this strength of character in His defiance of legalistic traditions. When the disciples were hungry one Sabbath Day, Jesus allowed them to pick heads of grain in a field and eat them. For this He was severely criticized by the Pharisees, but He wasn't ruffled by them (see Matthew 12:1-8). He

33

simply and strongly declared himself to be "lord of the sabbath" (v. 8).

Jesus became quite angry at the hypocrites He saw in the religious establishment of His day. He entered a synagogue on the Sabbath. "And behold, there was a man with a withered hand. And they asked him, 'Is it lawful to heal on the sabbath?' so that they might accuse him" (Matthew 12:10). Jesus wasn't taken aback by their threat. Rather, He showed them their hypocrisy, first through using a homey story from their everyday knowledge: "What man of you, if he has one sheep and it falls into a pit on the sabbath, will not lay hold of it and lift it out? Of how much more value is a man than a sheep! So it is lawful to do good on the sabbath" (vv. 11, 12). Then in the presence of all His detractors, He said to the man, " 'Stretch out your hand.' And the man stretched it out, and it was restored, whole like the other" (v. 13). This is not the ministry of a sissy!

Again, when He came to the temple and found the many tables of moneychangers and those who were selling pigeons for the sacrifices—and making unjust profits in the transactions—He was unafraid to overturn their tables and drive the cheaters out with a whip. (See Matthew 21:12.) He then declared to them: " 'My house shall be called a house of prayer'; but you make it a den of robbers" (v. 13). Again, these aren't the words of one who was afraid to be himself or afraid to offend others.

And He was so strong emotionally that He could die a horrible death without whimpering or cursing those who hung Him on the cross. So when such a Man proclaims, "Blessed are the meek," is He talking about a creature far different from himself?

No, He is not! He is speaking out of an attribute

34

that was fully developed in himself—and a characteristic that has far too often been misrepresented by those who don't want to humble themselves and become like Jesus Christ.

With this understanding of Jesus Christ, we can turn to the meaning given to the word *meek* in Greek literature prior to Jesus' time. This will give us additional help in understanding the kind of person Jesus was and what He wants us to be when He applies the term to us. Second, if we consult our own dictionaries, we will also come to an agreement of terms. According to the dictionary, meek means gentle, kind, courteous; merciful; free from self-will; piously humble and submissive; patient and unresentful.

Aristotle used the word to speak of a person who does not take the extreme course. For him, a meek man was neither an extravagant spender nor a penny-pinching miser; neither a coward nor a daredevil; neither an ultraconservative nor a radical. Aristotle's meek man would neither drive his car down the street like Al Unser in the Indy 500 nor like old Mr. Jones hugging the curb at 10 mph. Such a meek man would neither risk all his income by investing in a questionable manufacturing company nor put every dime of it in a bank account that paid a minimum rate of interest.

Meek was also a word ascribed to a wild horse that had been trained. The unbridled energy that had been unpredictably going off in all directions, often causing harm to human and horse, was now channeled and directed for predictable purposes. The result was an animal whose energies could be used for both work and enjoyment.

Sometimes people get a little shook when they

learn that the meek Jesus got angry on occasion. They misunderstand the nature of meekness. A meek man is one who can become angry at the right time and never become angry at the wrong time. Jesus got angry at hypocrisy, injustice, and blind stupidity. There are occasions when with force we must hear the words of Paul: "Be ye angry." Yet that anger is conditional: "Be ye angry, *and* sin not" (Ephesians 4:26, *KJV*). The anger of the Christian never comes in defense of his own petty setbacks, but over the issues with which the Son of God himself became indignant.

Therefore, if you are to be meek you must rule your emotions, not let your emotions rule you. You must live under discipline and experience the clear channeling of your energies. What applications there are for us!

You are meek when you fight the temptation to waste your time on trivialities or, on the other hand, when you refrain from spending every moment with "your nose to the grindstone" lest you cease to be a social being.

As a member of a small group, you learn to live with balance, not spending all your time alone or with the group.

As a social person involved with members of the opposite sex, your response is neither frozen nor boiling. After five dates with the same girl, a young man is not necessarily a meek person if he has not yet held her hand. Conversely, he is not meek if he has progressively tried to see how far he can go. Meekness does not mean the absence of passion, but the control of passion.

As an athlete, you are not meek if you never get roused up with the desire to win. Neither are you meek if you pop off all the time and become a sorehead about each loss.

As a businessman, you are not meek if you simply avoid the pressures of making your business more successful. Neither are you meek if you drive yourself beyond your physical or mental capacities.

In every situation, Jesus is telling us to be meek—to be controlled people. We are mistaken, however, if we assume this is all He means by the word *meek*. Jesus gives added meaning to the word when He says: "Come to me, all who labor and are heavy laden, and I will give you rest. Take my yoke upon you, and learn from me; for I am gentle and lowly in heart . . . " (Matthew 11:28, 29).

To be meek is not only to be controlled and disciplined, to be in the center between extremes; but also to be gentle.

Jesus shows us His gentleness in saying that when we come and take His yoke, He will treat us with kindness. His warning finger will not be constantly shaking at us and reminding us of our sins, failures, and inferiorities. He will not be yelling at us: "You dumb ox, now pull my load harder. Get up off the ground, you beast, or I'll put my gospel whip deeper into your flank."

He asks us to be gentle-spirited toward each other and to lay aside harsh attitudes and judgments, especially toward other believers. We don't give up our strength or dignity when we are kind, even as Jesus did not yield up His forceful personality to be gentle. It is not an "either/or" but a "both/and" situation.

Paul captured this truth quite well: "Be kind to one another, tenderhearted, forgiving one another, as God in Christ forgave you" (Ephesians 4:32). James also helps us understand more about this as-

37

pect of the word *meek:* "But the wisdom that comes from heaven is first of all pure and full of quiet gentleness. Then it is peace-loving and courteous. It allows discussion and is willing to yield to others; it is full of mercy and good deeds. It is wholehearted and straightforward and sincere" (James 3:17, *The Living Bible*).

Jesus' meekness led Him to live under the Father's control. His meekness not only showed His discipline and gentleness, but also His submission to the Father's will. Isaiah described this kind of meekness so well when he said:

> He was oppressed, and he was afflicted, yet he opened not his mouth; like a lamb that is led to the slaughter, and like a sheep that before its shearers is dumb, so he opened not his mouth (Isaiah 53:7).

Out of the example of Christ's own meekness, we also are given the call to live a meek life, a life submitted to God: "If any man would come after me, let him deny himself and take up his cross and follow me" (Mark 8:34).

Jesus' teaching on being meek is not just moral advice to all men. It is a quality present only among those who recognize their complete lack of resources to get into God's kingdom—the poor in spirit. And Jesus declares that after one has recognized his poverty and wept, he must then live in the dimension of always submitting his will to God. There are many "balanced" people in the world who are not Christians. They may be even-tempered people who live good lives, give money to the poor, and work for the oppressed—but they are not truly meek. The truly meek are those who, having trusted Christ, follow the pattern He set forth.

So it is not difficult now to see why Jesus said the meek shall inherit the earth. First, because they have placed their confidence in the Owner of all things. We are not so foolish as to suppose we can gain ultimate wealth and unlimited life on our own. We know God is the Source, and the day will come when we will receive that which only He can give.

Second, the meek inherit the earth because they can uniquely claim the world in which they operate. Not given to extremes, having their emotions under control, and being gentle in their treatment of others—all these put them in quiet command of themselves and eventually of their surroundings. They are not upset by flashes of emotion. They are not victimized by any personally motivated tyrannical attitudes. They and their world are in harmony. Possessing themselves, they possess their world!

The next time you overhear someone describing you, pray that he is saying you are meek; for then he will be calling you what Christ wants to call you. God's blessing always consists of two elements: (1) God approves your life; and (2) you are full of deep joy within because you are in direct alignment with God's will.

For this day, Jesus again holds out the promise: "Blessed are the meek, for they shall inherit the earth."

"Blessed are those who hunger and thirst for righteousness, for they shall be satisfied" (Matthew 5:6).

5

When You Hunger and Thirst for What Is Right

At some time or other, almost all of us believe that there's a universal hunger within humans to know God. Admittedly, in most people this craving seems to be only a dissatisfaction with their personal inability to reach perfection and a fear that there just might be Someone beyond themselves who can inflict punishment on them for doing wrong. But a craving to know God in an intimate, life-changing way isn't evident; nor is there much of a rush to find out who the true God might be.

Likewise, many people, especially those in the field of education, talk about the inner craving to gain knowledge. They claim this is especially alive in children and youth. Having, however, been a college student myself, I've discovered that at least the collegian's hunger for knowledge has been overestimated. Instructors presume it and college administrators assume it. And such presumptions and assumptions are probably necessary to bolster the egos of professors and to justify the larger college budgets proposed by administrators.

But sit where students sit, talk with them in the

dorm lounges, and visit with them in relaxed campus settings, and you'll make a discovery. Some honestly thirst for knowledge like a blotter absorbing water. (These students will be found in the science lab, the music practice room, or the college library.) But others appear more like ducks being doused with water, it seems impossible to saturate them. Knowledge doesn't penetrate. Some students are simply lazy; they'd rather loaf or sleep than study. Others seem to have come to college for entertainment, athletic purposes, or to make friends. And most need an occasional shove, prod, or even a threat to get them to keep drinking at the fountains of wisdom and knowledge.

Certainly Jesus found this to be true. He came with no naive assumptions that the majority of people, either in Palestine where He ministered or throughout the ages worldwide, were desperately longing to live right and enter the kingdom of God. People weren't standing in line to become His followers.

Of course, you'll always discover a remnant who desire to follow God's way. John made note of the fact that Jesus "came to his own home, [a possible reference to Christ's coming to his own hometown, Nazareth] and his own people received him not. But to all who received him, . . . he gave power to become children of God" (John 1:11, 12). This showed Jesus attracted followers, though not in droves.

In the Parable of the Sower, Jesus succinctly analyzed the types of people and their reactions to His call to discipleship. (See Matthew 13:1-9, 18-23.) A sower went out to sow. Some seed fell along the path and birds devoured it immediately. Some fell on rocky ground where there was not much soil.

Plants sprang up quickly but soon withered and died because of the scorching sun. Other seeds fell among thorns. The thorns grew faster than the plants and eventually choked them out. Finally some seed fell on good ground—and produced an abundant crop for harvesting.

Jesus said the first seeds didn't even have a chance. The evil one snatched the seeds away before they even germinated. The rocky ground was the person who superficially received the message of Christ, had a lot of emotional excitement generated within about the faith, but didn't have what it takes when the pressures and heat were turned on. The plants among the thorns started out okay, but when the cares and calls of the world came, they too succumbed. They wanted the delights of riches rather than the demands of discipleship.

But don't lose heart if you are trying to follow Christ's prescribed way of life. Don't think you are the only one going God's way. Don't get the "Elijah complex"—"Only I am left." There will always be those who sincerely seek after God, who are the good soil, and have a continual hunger and thirst after righteousness.

The question is: Are you one of this minority? The Beatitudes do not appeal to the masses. They appeal to a minority even among those who have initially "trusted Jesus Christ as their own personal Saviour." And the further one gets in the application of the Beatitudes, the smaller this minority seems to become.

No wonder Jesus said, "For the gate is narrow and the way is hard, that leads to life, and those who find it are few" (Matthew 7:14).

It is not a contradiction of the Beatitude, "Blessed

are those who hunger and thirst. . . ," when the apostle Paul summarizes the verdict of the Old Testament: "None is righteous, no, not one; no one understands, no one seeks for God. All have turned aside, together they have gone wrong; no one does good, not even one" (Romans 3:10-12).

Hunger for God begins after you realize the truth of Paul's statement. When you recognize He is speaking to you when He says, in essence: "Don't stand before God with platitudes about how anxiously you have sought after Him. You are not righteous and you have not sought after Him. The truth of the matter is more like that which Isaiah proclaimed, 'All we like sheep have gone astray; we have turned every one to his own way' (Isaiah 53:6)." It is only when one's lack of hunger is recognized that true hunger can really begin.

That is why Jesus did not make "blessed are those who hunger and thirst . . . " the first Beatitude. Prerequisite to that deep longing for God must be the realization of destitution in God's presence ("Blessed are the poor in spirit"), the open sense of brokenness ("Blessed are those who mourn"), and the entering into of a controlled, submitted life ("Blessed are the meek").

Yes, the entrance into the Kingdom is through faith in Jesus Christ, but you have to grow in the principles of the Kingdom until you naturally act like one of the Kingdom's subjects. As you grow, the Holy Spirit is wonderfully at work creating an intense hunger and thirst for the things of God. Beware if your life is not characterized by these deep longings to know Jesus Christ and be like Him. If that hunger and thirst is not there, turn back to the first Beatitude—"Blessed are the poor in spirit"—and begin there with a full confession of your need for the grace of God to bring deliverance from sin.

The hunger and thirst of which Jesus speaks is not the hunger that prompts you to run to a fast-food restaurant and order a hamburger and Coke at 10:30 p.m. The hunger and thirst Jesus means is that which is so severe that you feel life will cease unless its need is met. Jesus profoundly influences only men and women who are desperate.

Furthermore, in this Beatitude is a further clue to the whole theme of happiness or deep joy in life. In chapter 1 we discussed the concept that happiness is a by-product of our commitments, not the goal. Thus, we would agree with Martin Lloyd-Jones when he says:

> We are not to hunger and thirst after blessedness; we are not to hunger and thirst after happiness. But that is what most people are doing. We put happiness and blessedness as the one thing that we desire, and thus we always miss it; it always eludes us. According to the Scriptures, happiness is never something that should be sought directly; it is always something that results from seeking something else.

Unfortunately, far too many of us have been trapped into this world's approach to life. The quest for happiness has been made life's major goal. Happiness in business. Happiness in the home. Happiness in the community. Happiness by entertainment. Happiness by travel. Happiness by friendships. We put the cart before the horse. Instead of finding our delights in giving ourselves, we seek them in what we get for ourselves. Consequently, what we seek is like a vapor; it eludes us. We can't grasp it, yet we seek it all the more.

Or, we set our happiness goal on achieving a position. One young man, upon entering a Christian college, was filled with a consuming ambition to be student-body president. The motivation for this came from a deep psychological need to be approved by others. He lived with that goal for nearly 3 years until the May afternoon arrived for the vote tabulation to be announced. He had made it to the inner two, but the goal he had striven for was denied. A real touch of bitterness set in, not only against certain students (especially the winner and his friends), but even against God, who had evidently denied this fulfillment. Only later did he see that his preoccupation should have been on attaining the goals Jesus has set for human life.

Whenever we give priority to a goal that Jesus Christ has not established for us, we run the risk of fouling up our life. We are forever setting goals pertaining to what we want *to do;* Jesus is forever setting goals for us that tell us what *to be.* This is what makes the Beatitudes so contrary to the way most of us want to go—*doing* versus *being.* The way of Christ is to make us new beings, then the doing will follow. Being must come first!

The individual who is living in Jesus' life-style can cope with personal setbacks in reaching his own goals—broken dreams, financial adversity, physical misfortune, and even the sorrow of death. He can cope with these because he knows they are the result of temporary goals—but the abiding goals of a truly Christian life-style can never be taken away.

Barbara Jurgensen, in commenting on this Beatitude, asks:

Have you ever noticed how *The New English Bible* translates this verse? "How blest are those who hunger and thirst to see right prevail."

That isn't the same at all! Look, I know this world's in a sort of a mess and I know a lot of people have a lot of problems and I suppose somebody has to help them, but it doesn't have to be me! I don't want to get involved; I've got all I can do trying to be righteous myself.

Wow! An added demand. We must not only be righteous ourselves, but also be in the vanguard that promotes righteousness. We must be the "salt of the earth" and constantly counteract the corrupting forces in society. We must be instigators of righteousness rather than passive spectators who simply condemn evil.

Actually, who would expect less of himself? How could one be a seeker after inner righteousness without having some compulsion to see righteousness prevail in society? Yes, let's add this third dimension to the fourth Beatitude.

Jesus says we should be desperately hungry and thirsty for good conduct and to see the causes of right prevail. We must not be satisfied with a partial sampling of righteousness, but strive for the fullest dimension—all righteousness—even to the perfection of our character. Our Heavenly Father has said, "Be holy as I am holy." When we strive for this, we discover the deepest truth about righteousness: it can only be received. That's why Jesus Christ has become righteousness for us.

When righteousness becomes a central goal, against which all other goals pale into insignificance,

47

you will experience the inner dynamic of the presence of Jesus. God will put His approval on your deep yearning and an inner condition will grow in your heart—you "shall be satisfied."

Being right and doing right make life fulfilling. In fact, it's so fulfilling that Jesus didn't even have to attach any eternal element to the promised result of hungering and thirsting after righteousness. One's thirst and hunger are satisfied in the resultant inner attitude and outward acts.

You can't beat this Beatitude for producing some of life's most abiding and enriching satisfactions. God gives us, through Jesus Christ, all the righteousness we desire and all the satisfactions we can contain.

"Blessed are those who hunger and thirst for righteousness, for they shall be satisfied."

"Blessed are the merciful,
for they shall obtain mercy" (Matthew 5:7).

6

Giving Ourselves to Others

It seems one of the most difficult aspects of the Christian life is wrapped up in this Beatitude. Our religion, whether it's Christianity or not, basically wraps itself in ourselves. We soon notice this when we analyze our prayers. How often we pray for that which benefits us as individuals . . . and forget so much of the world which is in far greater need than we! We become acutely aware of all Christ has done—for us! Our doctrine of salvation is clear. We've accepted the Saviour by faith. We are kept by faith. We'll get into heaven because of our faith in Him. How difficult it is to change from a self-centered approach.

The Beatitudes we have considered thus far have dealt mainly with our relationship to Jesus Christ and the inner attitudes we develop. "Blessed are the poor in spirit"—those who sense their inner destitution and their inability to change themselves to become acceptable to God. We are utterly dependent on the grace of Christ to transform us; we have no righteousness of our own and absolutely no reason to boast. And that's the way it should be!

49

"Blessed are those who mourn." They too know the wretchedness of utter destitution. They cry to God. And He hears and transforms them. He provides the comforting assurance of forgiveness, so those who genuinely grieve over their inward bankruptcy are comforted. When tears of repentance flow, inward peace is produced. A grief too deep to be concealed, repentance and sorrow for sin, total dependence on God's resources, an honest attitude of brokenness before God—these bring inner joy, comfort, and peace as God comes to our aid and changes the situations over which we have been grieving. There is forgiveness, harmony, reconciliation, and deep joy.

"Blessed are the meek." They are not given to extremes. They know the great strength of the character of Christ—His courage and His zeal for right. They are gentle, kind, courteous, free from self-will, piously humble and submissive, and patient and unresentful—all the evidences of inner character. They rule their emotions, put away harsh attitudes, and know how to set priorities and live a balanced life.

"Blessed are those who hunger and thirst for righteousness." This is more than a craving for knowledge. It's a craving for the right application of knowledge, for moral excellence. It's a desire to follow God's way; an inner longing not only to know Christ but also to be like Him and to see right prevail within society. This is the outworking of the righteousness the Holy Spirit has inbred into our souls.

This interpretation comes closest to Jesus' emphasis in the next Beatitude: "Blessed are the merciful, for they shall obtain mercy." This Beatitude results from the inward condition developed by the other Beatitudes; it can't stand alone. But it doesn't develop that inward condition; it's the outward manifestation of it. It's the way a person expresses his inner condition by outward acts. It's the condition of the heart that James would say is shown by outward evidence. He illustrated this by the life of Abraham: "You see that faith was active along with his works, and faith was completed by works" (James 2:22).

This is the Beatitude of the Good Samaritan. This is the Beatitude of "love your neighbor." It demonstrates that all the preceding ones have caught fire within one's spirit, and that Jesus Christ lives within. It shows you are living the Christ life.

What is mercy? Forbearance and compassion shown by one person to another. It is being willing to forgive, to help those in need who either can't or won't reciprocate, to perform acts of compassion and kindness toward suffering fellow creatures—to act like Jesus Christ acted toward needy people.

The Lord set the example for us in showing mercy. On two different occasions, two blind men called out to Him, "Have mercy on us" (Matthew 9:27; 20:30, 31). The Canaanite woman with the demon-possessed daughter didn't know much about Jesus, but she knew enough to cry to Him, "Have mercy on me, O Lord" (Matthew 15:22). This plea for mercy was echoed by another concerned parent—a father who wanted Jesus to deliver his demon-possessed son (Matthew 17:15). Ten lepers heard about Him and came to Him, calling loudly, "Jesus, Master, have mercy on us" (Luke 17:13).

How did Jesus get this reputation for being merciful? Do people come to you and address you distinctly as a person who has mercy? Jesus was ad-dressed with requests for mercy because His life was such an obvious demonstration of it.

Three times the Gospels state specifically that in His ministry He had compassion on crowds. For the leper in the terminal stages of his disease, Jesus was "moved with compassion." He stretched out His hand, touched him, and restored him (Mark 1:41, *KJV*). The widow of Nain, who was accompanying her dead son to the grave site, was seen by Jesus, and "he had compassion on her" (Luke 7:13).

When we look at the Beatitudes, we see this is the way Christ is. He is merciful. Not only do His deeds reflect mercy, but His teachings also show how much He desires this trait in His followers. Note the following four major illustrations of mercy Jesus gives us.

The Parable of the Good Samaritan (Luke 10:25-37) tells us to show mercy whenever the situation calls for it. The emphasis is not on the Good Samaritan's saying to himself, "How many good deeds can I perform today?" He didn't have a boy scout checklist of daily good deeds. And no one else even knew about the sacrifice he had made. Rather, the whole point of the story is that if, while you are doing your regular duties, someone comes to you for help, stop. Drop everything, even what you are legitimately doing, and come to his assistance. He sacrifices nothing at all who does the will of God.

Another parable of mercy is that of the two debtors (Matthew 18:23-35). The first debtor owed the king 10,000 talents (roughly $20 million). His request for leniency to the king was so pitiful the king canceled the debt.

The second debtor owed the first debtor 100 denarii (half the amount it would have taken to feed the 5,000, or one-third of the cost of the alabaster ointment that the woman anointed Jesus with prior to His death). One hundred denarii was only about $20 or 40 days' salary. Even though the first debtor's debt had been canceled, he refused to have mercy on the second debtor and threw him into prison.

What is Jesus teaching here about mercy? How is this story different from the Parable of the Good Samaritan? Jesus is simply saying the first debtor was encumbered with a debt he could never pay; it was an impossible amount. This is what our debt is to God. We always fall short of meeting His demands. We can never do enough to satisfy God's conditions. We can only cry for forgiveness and ask Him to deal with us in mercy. God honors our repentance and cancels what we owe.

The second debtor is our fellowman. If we do not forgive him when he asks, God will not forgive us. The bestowal of God's mercy on us is not only so we might have our debt canceled, but also that His Spirit might rub off on us and His pattern of mercy become ours.

We must practice mercy toward each other. To harbor anything against anyone—fellow employee, boss, family member, neighbor, church member, whomever—is contrary to the doctrine and Spirit of Christ. We do not give up our right to disagree with others on issues when we practice mercy—certainly Jesus had significant disagreements with persons around Him—but we do give up any spirit of animosity or hardness and anything contrary to mercy.

The Parable of the Good Samaritan is an illustration of how we should show mercy to those in need—even if we do not know them. The Parable of the Two Debtors shows us mercy is also to be extended toward those with whom we have interpersonal relations. Forgiveness is a quality of mercy.

The third and fourth illustrations of mercy show its importance as a criterion of judgment in the final day.

Luke 16:19-31 records the story of the rich man and Lazarus. The major sin of the rich man was that he failed to practice mercy. If there ever was a teaching of Jesus that condemned the pursuit of money for its own sake, this is it. Anyone who collects money and does not use it to help God's children fails to practice mercy and will be cast into hell.

This rich man was not sentenced to hell for something he had done. He had not ordered Lazarus removed. He hadn't kicked him or been deliberately cruel. While he may have feasted sumptuously every day, he hadn't tried to starve Lazarus; he'd been kind enough to let him eat the garbage. The wrongdoing of the rich man was a sin of omission. He had never noticed Lazarus. He had thought it was perfectly natural for him to live in luxury while Lazarus lived off the crumbs.

No wonder the rich man could not enter heaven. He would not have been at home there. Jesus Christ, the King of heaven, left luxury to save beggars, so He and the rich man had nothing in common. The rich man would have felt out of place in heaven.

The clear teaching of this incident is meant to affect our own personal goals. Our eternal future depends not on how much money or material comforts we have, but on whether or not we are using them to help people like Lazarus. If we lack mercy, we will end up living for ourselves and dying by ourselves—without God!

The fourth illustration of mercy is the Parable of the Sheep and the Goats (Matthew 25:31-46). In this teaching, Jesus clearly emphasizes the importance of mercy in the lives of His followers. He singles out six ways mercy can be practiced: feed the hungry, give drink to the thirsty, welcome the stranger, clothe the naked, and visit the sick and those in prison. These very simple things we often find so difficult because our energies are invested in doing something "great" for the Lord. Yet, there is nothing greater than doing His will.

It is these nameless, unremembered acts of kindness and love God wants us to do. The tremendous truth of this parable is that those who do these acts of mercy have no idea that they are doing these things unto Christ. They simply do them because they need to be done.

"The merciful . . . shall obtain mercy." Jesus is not saying, "All those who do good deeds will enter heaven." This Beatitude on mercy is part of a larger whole. The first four Beatitudes stress the kind of relationship we must have with God—we must be poor in spirit, mourning, meek, and hungry. As we enter this dimension, our relationship with God spills over into our relationships with others.

The merciful will obtain mercy. Without seeking it, mercy will return to the merciful. They will hear Christ's words in the Parable of the Sheep and the Goats: "Come, O blessed of my Father, inherit the kingdom prepared for you from the foundation of the world; for I was hungry and you gave me food, I was thirsty and you gave me drink, I was a stranger and you welcomed me, I was naked and you clothed me, I was sick and you visited me, I was in prison and you came to me" (Matthew 25:34-36).

If you want God to approve your present life and to bless you, then be merciful.

"Blessed are the pure in heart,
for they shall see God" (Matthew 5:8).

7

Being Crystal Clear Within

Many of us look back at high school physical education classes with a certain amount of embarrassment. Remember those gymnastic routines? Hoisting oneself up on the double rings? muscles and rings quivering? tight muscles all the next day?

Or, remember the rope dangling from the gymnasium ceiling? Those 20 or 25 feet up looked like a mile! The art of rope climbing not only meant getting to the top but also doing it in the shortest possible time. The ones who did it in the shortest time got the best grades.

How embarrassing to struggle to even get up on the rope! No matter how tightly you gripped the rope or how you wrapped your legs around it, you just could never make it to the top! "Top!" you say. "Would you believe less than halfway up?" And the harder you tried, the lower you slid. The whole effort was usually such an embarrassment you vowed, once out of that gym class, you'd give up rope climbing for life. And so far you have kept your promise!

The Beatitude, "Blessed are the pure in heart," may strike you in much the same way as rope climbing does the amateur rope climber. That is, you say this activity may be okay for others, but it is definitely not for me.

Is this statement of Jesus, for the vast majority of us, filled with futility? Is it the Mount Everest of ethics and relatedness to God? From our vantage point in the valley miles below, the whole thing is nice to talk about, but no one seriously considers the possibility of doing it!

After all, even Solomon said: "Who can say, 'I have made my heart clean; I am pure from my sin'?" (Proverbs 20:9). Jeremiah also testified: "The heart is deceitful above all things, and desperately corrupt; who can understand it?" (Jeremiah 17:9). Even Jesus acknowledged: "Out of the heart of man, come evil thoughts, fornication, theft, murder, adultery, coveting, wickedness, deceit, licentiousness, envy, slander, pride, foolishness" (Mark 7:21, 22). These are strong words—and the ultimate contrast to the words of this Beatitude.

Thus, these words of Jesus, "Blessed are the pure in heart," sear across our soul and our conscience. With them comes the instant recognition that we have utterly failed God by not being pure. Furthermore, since Christ's words have not been kept, the haunting possibility, "You shall *not* see God," strikes deep into our minds.

Failure to be pure in mind is hell. John, in Revelation, solemnly warns: "But as for the cowardly, the faithless, the polluted, as for murderers, fornicators, sorcerers, idolaters, and all liars, their lot shall be in the lake that burns with fire and brimstone, which is the second death" (Revelation 21:8). And again, he says, "Outside are the dogs and sorcerers and fornicators and murderers and idolaters, and every one who loves and practices falsehood" (22:15).

It is the laser light of this Beatitude, "Blessed are the pure in heart," that causes even the most righteous in our community to fall down as Isaiah; for both Isaiah and the righteous, when hearing of the absolute purity and holiness of the Lord of hosts, must recognize how far short of God's standard even they have come. All must confess: "Woe is me! For I am lost . . . " (Isaiah 6:5). So what chance have we? We are like amateur rope climbers. We'll never make it. Oh, the despair of it all. Why even try?

All these Scripture passages flash through our mind and consciousness as we hear the words of Christ, "Blessed are the pure in heart." We would sorrowfully turn away from Him with deepest weeping and rendering of spirit. The knowledge that we would like to be what He asks, but we can never reach it, is so painful.

The only thing that keeps us from utter despair is knowing Christ never lays burdens on His disciples that they cannot bear. His yoke is easy; His burden is light (Matthew 11:30). He is unlike the religious hypocrites He described who "bind heavy burdens hard to bear, and lay them on men's shoulders; but they themselves will not move them with their finger" (Matthew 23:4). We have One who not only is *touched* with the feeling of our infirmities" (Hebrews 4:15, *KJV*), but who also, according to Isaiah, "*took* our infirmities" (Matthew 8:17).

So when we come to the Beatitude, "Blessed are the pure in heart," we must drop our verdict that it cannot be achieved. Rather, we must listen to our Lord who says this can and must be done in our lives.

Think of it! Jesus is saying you can be pure! Pure from envy. Pure from hatred. Pure from lust. You can be free from every sin in your life and continually stand in God's presence as a pure person! You do not have to go on being enslaved by whatever is binding you. You can be loosed from it. You can be pure in heart. By heart, the Bible means the center of your person—your mind, will, and emotions—all can be pure. How?

Let us note the careful progression of the Beatitudes because it provides a crucial clue to the means whereby one can attain personal purity. The first three Beatitudes express a consciousness of need on our part. We are so destitute we recognize only God can give us the Kingdom. We are so grieved over our destitution only God can comfort us. This destitution and grieving bring us to the place of meekness—the confession of our complete submission to God. Only then can God give us the earth. The destitute, grieving, submissive person desperately desires God and His righteousness. And God satisfies that earnest desire.

What is the consequence? The man who is destitute has been in the place of the man who needs mercy, therefore, he knows how to give mercy. The first and fifth Beatitudes match: "Blessed are the poor in spirit"—"Blessed are the merciful." The person whose will is submitted to God and is gentle is prepared for the work of making peace. The third and seventh Beatitudes match: "Blessed are the meek"—"Blessed are the peacemakers." The person who grieves or mourns over his lostness, who deeply and openly repents of his sin, has met God's first requirement for purity of heart. The second and the sixth Beatitudes match: "Blessed are those who mourn"—"Blessed are the pure in heart."

One writer has compared the fourth Beatitude to

the summit of a mountain: The first three Beatitudes show the way up to the realization of God; the fifth through the seventh show the consequences of that realization.

Those who grieve become the pure in heart! Did not David find this true in his own experience? His great penitential Psalm 51 reveals this. He cries, mourns, and grieves over his sin. In that complete breaking, the Spirit burns the possibility of the light of a new day into his heart, and he cries: "Purge me with hyssop, and I shall be clean; wash me, and I shall be whiter than snow" (Psalm 51:7). Remember, this is a man who has committed adultery, deliberately had the woman's husband sent to the front line of battle so he would be killed, while at the same time permitting other brave warriors to lose their lives with him. Consequently, the illegitimate child of this adulterous union dies. Then this man says, "I shall be clean; wash me, and I shall be whiter than snow."

The plant of purity is watered with the tears of repentance. The plant of continued purity is watered by the tears of continued repentance. Hear the words of the apostle on this subject:

> If we walk in the light, as he is in the light, we have fellowship with one another, and the blood of Jesus his Son cleanses [purifies] us from all sin. If we say we have no sin, we deceive ourselves, and the truth is not in us. If we confess our sins, he is faithful and just, and will forgive our sins and cleanse [purify] us from all unrighteousness" (1 John 1:7-9).

How do we stay pure in heart? Note these laws:

One: Never, never let a single sin in your life go unconfessed for longer than the day in which it was committed. Bring that sin to God and confess it to Him. If you have wronged others through the sin, ask their forgiveness and correct what needs to be remedied.

Two: If you find yourself repeating the same sin over and over, keep confessing it over and over. Be careful not to be glib in such a confession simply as a cover-up to do it again. Confession is not just mouthing words; it is contriteness of heart and brokenness of spirit. Continued sorrow for the sin will help break its power. Coldness of heart perpetuates sin.

Note carefully Jesus' answer to Peter's question in Matthew 18: " 'Lord, how often shall my brother sin against me, and I forgive him? As many as seven times?' Jesus said to him, 'I do not say to you seven times, but seventy times seven' " (vv. 21, 22). If Jesus required this much forgiveness for man's repetitive sin against man, then how much more is His divine forgiveness given to us? With repetitive sin, get clean, get clean, get clean! Your prayers of confession will soon turn to praise for deliverance.

Three: You have a further responsibility beyond that of confession. Paul says to Timothy: "So shun youthful passions and aim at righteousness, faith, love, and peace, along with those who call upon the Lord from a pure heart" (2 Timothy 2:22). Paul is saying that purity of heart never comes if you wait idly for it to seize you. You cannot walk in the gutter of life. You must use all your willpower to avoid sin.

Four: As you do your best, God will help you. Purity of heart is desired by God and you. It will never be attained by your effort alone or by God's sovereign action alone. The Scriptures say: *"Draw near* to God and he will draw near to you. Cleanse your hands, you sinners, and purify your minds" (James 4:8). Again, the Word tells us: *"Work out your own salvation* with fear and trembling; for *God is at work in you,* both to will and to work for his good pleasure" (Philippians 2:12, 13).

As you "cleanse your hands," you will find Jesus speaking to you as He did to the disciples in John 15:3, "You are already made clean [pure] by the word which I have spoken to you." You will realize that "Christ loved [you] and gave himself up for [you], that he might sanctify [you], having cleansed [you] by the washing of water with the word, that he might present [you] to himself in splendor, without spot or wrinkle or any such thing, that [you] might be holy and without blemish" (Ephesians 5:25-27).

In summary, if you want to be pure in heart, do the following:

One: Confess your sin the day it occurs.

Two: Confess repeated sin each time, with a contrite heart.

Three: Do all within your power to live purely.

Four: God is at work in you. The Holy Spirit has resources for you according to your desire for them.

As you and God work together, as you draw near to Him and He draws near to you, your fellowship will intensify in meeting God through prayer and in the study of Scripture.

The pure in heart shall see God. This is not just a future reality, it is now! Sin obstructs the vision of God from your life. Sin drives you further and further from the light of the Father's house. Sin focuses your attention on that which is less than God. Sin calls your attention to forbidden things, forbidden pleasures, forbidden attitudes. You will never see God or perceive His will without the purity that results from obedience to Him.

In each of our eyes there is an intricate device designed for cleansing—the tear duct. When a foreign particle gets on the surface of the eyeball, the tear duct goes to work producing a liquid to help float away the extraneous substance. There can be no lasting sight without the watering of the tear duct or the moisture that coats the eye.

When you first experience the forgiveness of sins, you find a cleanness in Christ that results from His work and your acknowledgment of your sins. He places the Holy Spirit into your life, like the tear duct in the eye. When a foreign material enters in, the Holy Spirit is there to wash it away. But spiritual laws do not correspond to biological laws in every respect; for the Holy Spirit, unlike the tear duct gland, will not work automatically. You must ask.

Purity of heart, like purity of physical eyesight, does not mean you never get foreign material into your heart—for there is no avoiding that! Purity is in the continual washing away of foreign particles. No wonder Jesus links purity to sight: "Blessed are the pure in heart, for they shall see God."

"Blessed are the peacemakers,
for they shall be called sons of God" (Matthew 5:9).

8

Peacemakers

A common problem with a verse of this type is that its meaning is so evident that we quickly glide past it to get to more inspiring or penetrating truths. Who would linger long on the phrase "Blessed are the peacemakers" unless he is an avowed pacifist?

Of course, the trait of being a peacemaker is to be highly desired. That seems obvious. But most of us think we already have it! We usually define it by looking at its opposites: warmongers, agitators, rioters. Who but the revolutionary wants to be these?

Peacemakers. That's us! After all, hasn't there been at least one situation in our lives when we openly advocated peace—between nations, between individuals! Possibly we've even stepped in between two parties who were having a quarrel. Our presence brought peace—at least temporarily.

We suspect that down deep, each of us credits to himself a gentle streak of disposition that—no matter how mean and gruff we may appear to be—helps us establish a good feeling about ourselves. Basically, we are a peaceable sort of person. We like to live at peace with others and help them to be peaceable like ourselves.

Yet, if we are to "be called sons of God" because of our peacemaking attitudes and activities, it seems there's a lot more to consider.

First, let's take a good, close look at the life of the Proponent of this Beatitude.

When Jesus was born, the angels announced to all: "Peace on earth." Bringing God's peace to men seemed to be a prominent purpose of the Incarnation. When Jesus had nearly completed His earthly course, He said to His disciples: "Peace I leave with you; my peace I give to you" (John 14:27); and, "I have said this to you, that in me you may have peace" (16:33). Several times after His resurrection, He greeted His people with the words: "Peace be unto you" (Luke 24:36; John 20:21, 26, *KJV*). Thus, it can be seen from the Gospels that one of the central concerns of Jesus was bringing peace. Indeed, He felt He had accomplished that mission. May we now suggest specific ways in which Jesus served as a Maker of peace?

First, only the person who has peace within himself can make peace. Jesus never had hostility toward the Father; therefore, He is fully qualified to speak to others about peace between God and man. Jesus, while differing from others, never held hostility against them. He loved even His enemies; even those who nailed Him to the cross and mocked Him. He said, "Father, forgive them. . . ." He is fully qualified to speak of peace among men!

A peacemaker is one who has ended conflict with God by removing that which causes enmity between God and men—human rebellion and sin. He has also done everything within his power to end conflict between himself and his fellowmen. In regard to the latter, it may be necessary to judge the ideas and actions of a fellowman, but never does this involve hating the man himself or judging his soul. That is God's task alone. You cannot make peace unless you are at peace.

Second, Jesus made peace by making victory. As a peacemaker, He knew what needed to be defeated. Through His life, death, and resurrection, He defeated Satan and ended the power of sin and death. He did not compromise with sinners but engaged in peacemaking—He reconciled His enemies to God by His death. Paul declares: "And you, who once were estranged and hostile in mind, doing evil deeds, he has now reconciled in his body of flesh by his death, in order to present you holy and blameless and irreproachable before him" (Colossians 1:21). Jesus takes away the enmity not by temporarily submerging differences, but by taking away the cause of the quarrel, sin itself, and triumphing over it.

It is from the life of Jesus Christ, both in the manner He lived and the principles He taught, that we discover the true meaning of being a peacemaker.

As peacemakers, we must learn to follow the example of Christ. Peace was His end result, but peaceableness was not always His means. The peacemaker has as his objective, peace; but his methods to attain peace may not necessarily be pleasant ones.

Jesus said: "Do not think that I have come to bring peace on earth; I have not come to bring peace, but a sword. For I have come to set a man against his father, and a daughter against her mother, and a daughter-in-law against her mother-in-law; and a man's foes will be those of his own household" (Matthew 10:34-36). He is not here talking of the end, but the means. If Jesus had to drink the cup of suffering and bear the cross to make peace; if He had to be hounded by men and take issue with them to the point of death for their sins; if He had to do all this to make peace; then consider that you are not above your Lord. Your efforts to make peace will also be met by misunderstanding, jealousy, and rejection.

This Beatitude has often been thought of as referring only to bringing peace between men. But surely, if Jesus is the pattern, it must also mean bringing men into peaceful relationships with God. If you have tried to bring someone to God, you know what rejection and hatred can be. Because you experience this, it does not mean you are not being a peacemaker—for you are only following your Lord.

Jesus is an example for us in three ways. First, He has no enmity with the Father or hatred for man. Second, He kept peace as an objective while knowing it would come through hardship and giving His life. Third, there is no selfishness in Him.

The writer of Proverbs states: "A wrathful man stirreth up strife" (15:18, *KJV*); "Where there is no talebearer, strife ceaseth" (26:20, *KJV*); and, "He that is of a proud heart stirreth up strife" (28:25, *KJV*).

None of these remarks characterizes Christ, and they should not characterize us. Applied to Christian community, these proverbs give us five antidotes to strife or five means of maintaining peace among ourselves: (1) let selfish anger and sullenness cease; (2) let each person keep his mouth sealed, opening it only in a Biblically approved way; (3) let each proud and vain person quit being that way; (4) let each person who has hatred or who has held a grudge against someone confess it and drop it; (5) let each one who is sinning quit, because the person whose life is marked by constant strife is constantly sinning as well.

We are enjoined by the apostle Paul: "Let nothing be done through strife" (Philippians 2:3, *KJV*).

Out of the development of these inner characteristics we produce the ability to be peacemakers. As peacemakers, we are thrust into a society of strife. We become God's go-betweens, settling the quarrels and conflicts that tear people apart from each other. The peacemaker stands in the gap. "Blessed"— approved and recognized by God—"are the peacemakers."

A peacemaker, as Christ proclaimed, is not simply a diplomat who sits at a conference negotiating settlements among nations. While that is an honorable and needed profession, we have already noted that Jesus applies this Beatitude to common folk like us and that such Beatitudes come in "domino" fashion. This domino, "Blessed are the peacemakers," stands in front of some others.

The person who makes peace, therefore, has already seen the barriers between himself and God disappear. He has been destitute (poor), grieved over sin (mourned), and become submissive to God (meek). This has resulted in a deeper hunger and thirst for righteousness. As he begins reaching for it, his poverty of spirit is translated into mercy toward others. As he experiences what it is to be grieved and repentant over sins, he can be pure in heart. As he submits himself to God, God uses him as a peacemaker.

So, you see, the peacemaker is preeminently a

member of Christ's kingdom, not simply a servant of human government. He is not necessarily a negotiator, because if this is what Jesus meant by the word, He himself failed to fulfill it.

Second, a peacemaker is not simply one who refrains from taking sides. In other words, Jesus is not placing a blessing on all those who stay neutral when issues demand they be otherwise. One of the greatest dangers in society and in the church comes from those who imagine they can best serve their group by never taking a clear stand on anything.

If a peacemaker is one who never takes sides, Jesus failed miserably. He was one of the most controversial people of His age, or any age! He took sides with two men against a whole town of people who had elevated the value of their pigs above the value of a man. He took sides against the Pharisees, Herodians, Sadducees, high priest, chief priests, elders, scribes, and family. He was for right against wrong, righteousness against sin, and truth against expediency.

If you expect to be a peacemaker among people and imagine you can do it by being a chameleon with your convictions, standing on neutral ground between the issues, or taking the safe side of the opinion of the majority, you certainly aren't following Christ's pattern for making peace.

Third, the peacemaker is not necessarily a compromiser. There is a difference between the "never-take-sides" person and the compromiser. The former stands aloof from the struggles of opposites, but the latter attempts to knock off the sharp edges of the combatants so they are palatable to each other. The compromiser says, "If you give up A, he will give up

B, and while neither of you particularly like C, at least you can agree."

There are times when compromise is essential. Let's face it: we could not live long in society without it. Nations must practice this art and so must individuals. Yet, there are times when compromise is terribly wrong and immoral.

If "blessed are the peacemakers" could read "blessed are the compromisers," Pilate would be in heaven today. And those compromisers who are presently at work on the international church scene, trying to formulate beliefs that all people can accept by diluting such great truths as the Virgin Birth and the bodily resurrection of Jesus Christ, would soon be awarded the left- and right-hand seats in the kingdom of Christ.

Well, if the peacemaker is not a diplomat, a person who always stays neutral, or a compromiser—just what is he? and what does he do?

Jesus not only wants peaceable people, He also wants peacemakers—not just those who wish for peace, but who work for it. He is calling common people to the task. It isn't a work reserved for diplomats and it isn't necessarily never taking sides or being a compromiser. To be a peacemaker is to, first, with Christ, be at peace with God and not hold any hatred against men. It is, second, to strive for peace as the end while recognizing that the means to that end may be painful and result in immediate opposition rather than peace. And, third, it is to live unselfishly.

Is there something you need to make peace with today? Is there someone with whom you need to make peace? God sought to reconcile you; should you not seek to reconcile your brother?

71

You will be called sons of God. No wonder! The Father himself is the "God of peace who brought again from the dead our Lord Jesus . . . " (Hebrews 13:20). The Son is the Prince of Peace. It is in the name of the Son that the apostle declared: "Now may the Lord of peace himself give you peace at all times in all ways" (2 Thessalonians 3:16).

God approves the peacemaker—that's enough! "Blessed are the peacemakers," who know peace within themselves and who promote it among mankind. "They shall be called sons of God."

*"Blessed are those who are persecuted for righteousness' sake,
for theirs is the kingdom of heaven" (Matthew 5:10).*

9

When You Are Clobbered
for What Is Right

In a sense, the Beatitudes are like the Panama
Canal. The canal consists of a series of water locks or
links through which a large ship passes from one
ocean to the other. The ship must remain in each
water lock until the water has risen to a high enough
level to float the ship on to the next lock. The locks
are interlinked and the ship must pass through all of
them in sequence if it is to safely journey from the
Pacific to the Atlantic Ocean, or vice versa.

The Beatitudes are interlocking. For the "blessed" life, you must pass through each one; maybe not
in the exact order, but pretty much in sequence.
None can be bypassed. The man who begins going
through them is marked by poverty of spirit. When
he comes out at the other end, he faces the definite
possibility of being persecuted. He comes to God
hunting for reality; he goes away being hunted by
others. What accounts for this transformation?

You can explain it only by knowing the Beatitudes
contain some interlocking chains that properly develop the man of God. The inevitable result of following God's orders for your life and living by a

righteous standard, is rejection by those who reject God or who aren't committed to the changes in life-style Jesus Christ produces. Simply put, you are sub-ject to persecution by those whose lives are exposed by the new concepts governing your pattern of liv-ing.

Let's make this clear: The *goal* of the follower of Christ is not persecution, but the *result* often is. The person who goes out deliberately trying to find someone to persecute him will only be persecuted for his own stupidity. Jesus did not pronounce a blessing on such people, but on those who are perse-cuted because of righteousness.

Quite frequently we meet people who have what is known by the psychological term "persecution complex." They continually feel that because they specialize in right living and they see many others specializing in evil, most of the world lives to oppose them. This is a self-inflicted persecution. And if the opposition seems to come because of a relationship between their religious faith and their actions, they assume they are being persecuted because they are Christians. Unfortunately, their persecution is the result of their asking for it, or of their own invention. Simply because others are unenthusiastic about your expressions of personal religion, or they laugh at your list of dos and don'ts, gives you no justification for being persecuted.

Jesus really didn't have such situations in mind. Those about whom He spoke were genuinely dis-criminated against or physically harmed, not be-cause they desired to be or looked for it, but because their faith in Him so transformed their lives that those around them were severely threatened and uncomfortable. By outward, sometimes violent, op-

74

position they desired to eliminate such religious influence. It is the ingrained result of the first seven Beatitudes that produces the reactions stated in the eighth.

The goal of the true disciple is stated in the fourth Beatitude: "Blessed are those who hunger and thirst after righteousness." Three connected means of righteousness are given in the first three Beatitudes: (1) The destitute man (poor in spirit) seeks a righteousness not of himself, for he recognizes he has nothing. He needs what the reformers called *an alien righteousness.* (2) The destitute person breaks before God in repentance (he mourns) because of how far short he has come of ever manifesting the righteousness of God that He requires. (3) The destitute and repentant person becomes submissive to God (meek) and acquires the discipline to act in a manner that pleases God.

These three means to righteousness are then followed by three consequences of righteousness: (1) Mercy comes from the one who has needed mercy. (2) Purity of heart comes out of the one who has been repentant, who has mourned over his sins. (3) Peacemaking naturally follows in the life of the one who has learned to be submissive and disciplined before God.

Too often our concept of Christianity involves a break between the first seven Beatitudes and the eighth, because we never dream the Beatitudes produce revolutionaries. But the connection of the eighth Beatitude to the preceding ones is central in Jesus' logic. His teaching, therefore, about being poor, mourners, meek, hungry, merciful, pure, and peacemakers does not result in namby-pamby individuals so filled with "good-Joe" piety that no one in his right mind would even take the time to throw a stick at them.

If there is no persecution for righteousness' sake directed against you at this present time, maybe you ought to do some self-examination. First, thank God you have an exemption from the rule. Second, go back over the first seven Beatitudes and inventory your life in the light of them. Your motive—let us repeat—is not to suffer persecution for doing what is right, but to be like Jesus Christ. Persecution will be the result of such a commitment. Surely this is the idea Paul declared, "Indeed all who desire to live a godly life in Christ Jesus will be persecuted" (2 Timothy 3:12).

You may ask, "But who in the world would want to persecute little old me?" That's precisely the point. No one will persecute little *old* you, but a host of people will persecute the *new* you that has Christ dominating within. Look at what Jesus said: "If the world hates you, know that it has hated me before it hated you. If you were of the world, the world would love its own; but because you are not of the world, but I chose you out of the world, therefore the world hates you. Remember the word that I said to you, 'A servant is not greater than his master.' If they persecuted me, they will persecute you" (John 15:18-20).

From whom will persecution come? Look for it from at least five sources, for they are the places from which Christ's own persecution came.

First, Christ's family misunderstood His mission and voiced that misunderstanding. Your family might persecute you because of your identification with Christ which produces a standard of conduct that might make theirs look second-rate. For those from Christian homes this has little meaning, but for some this is a very real thing. Often the greatest opposition comes from family members who don't appreciate your new way of life. It stands as a condemnation to their sinful manner of living. It is a contrast to what they have accepted as religious truth; therefore, they resist—sometimes by verbal arguments, harmful physical force, or ostracism. In blessing you, Jesus says He approves you even though your family doesn't.

Second, your friends may persecute you. Jesus' hometown people rejected Him. At one point in His ministry, His friends said He was crazy (Mark 3:21, *The Living Bible*). They seemed excited about His good works—up to a point. They wanted no comparisons!

Your friends may not persecute you if they are all Christians, but some Christians may pay a price in persecution from friends for taking their stand for right living. In fact, what keeps many from witnessing is this very fear of being persecuted by friends.

Let us illustrate how persecution works. Take a college student who is always knocking the top off the grade curve. That student is seeking knowledge, not persecution. He winds up getting both! Why? Because others are made uncomfortable when their lack of knowledge and discipline shows up. (We are taking for granted that the top student is not getting persecuted because he is conceited!)

Also, some friends are exceedingly uncomfortable around someone who aims at strict honesty in all aspects of living. That's what Christianity produces. A new creature in Christ is an honest person toward the world. And such righteous living can't be tolerated by many. Therefore, the Christian gets taunted about being a goody-goody even though he is only attempting to demonstrate that which is operative within.

The third source of persecution for Jesus was members of the religious establishment. It is interesting to compare the seventh and eighth Beatitudes in this relationship. The members of Christ's kingdom will suffer persecution, but nowhere in the Scriptures are they given any authority for inflicting it. They are to be peacemakers—that is, their aim is to reconcile men to God and to their fellowmen. A religious establishment becomes corrupt when it pursues a policy of persecuting its opposition rather than proclaiming the gospel of peace.

It may be that those in your religious group are genuinely committed, therefore, they will not persecute anyone in the group. However, many Christians are misunderstood, verbally maligned, and repudiated by other so-called Christians because of their stand for Christian ideals and conduct. Some religious leaders say their greatest opposition comes not from sinners but from people claiming allegiance to Jesus Christ. How can this be?

A fourth source of Christ's opposition was the government. We are in a different political system than He and therefore are not experiencing this level of persecution. Contrast our experience, however, with that of Christians in the Middle Ages or with Christians in China today.

The fifth avenue of persecution against Jesus was given in the generalized title of "the world." For us, this is where we work, live, and have social associations. Our right-living activities will find us both making peace—leading some to the Lord—and experiencing persecution, rejection, lies, and slander.

But don't give up. Jesus gives a great promise to

those who are persecuted for doing what is right. He gave the same promise to the person who is poor in spirit. It is a continuation of the results of following Beatitude living. "Blessed are those who are persecuted for righteousness' sake, for theirs is the kingdom of heaven."

These Christians know the reigning power of Jesus Christ. They sense they are not restricted by time-space measurements. They have God in their lives, and their present and future are wrapped up in a relationship to Him. They have far more than their persecutors possess. And in contrast to the rejection and tormenting of their persecutors, those who are persecuted discover divine acceptance. They live in kinship to the One who was "despised and rejected by men; a man of sorrows, and acquainted with grief" (Isaiah 53:3). Acceptance by God far outweighs rejection by men.

When faced with opposition for living righteously before men, remember the words of the Originator of righteousness: "Blessed [approved by God] are those who are persecuted for righteousness' sake, for theirs is the kingdom of heaven." Acceptance of the promise overbalances even the severest persecution.

*"Blessed are you when men revile you
and persecute you and utter all kinds of evil
against you falsely on my account.
Rejoice and be glad,
for your reward is great in heaven" (Matthew 5:11, 12).*

10

When You Are Accused Falsely
for Your Faith

A close relationship exists between being "perse-cuted for righteousness' sake" and being persecuted "on my [Christ's] account." Often there's overlap-ping. Since the Christian is known for good works, those who are troubled by such good works will be antagonistic toward the person's faith as well.

But the Christian can't automatically say he is being persecuted for being a Christian—unless, of course, it is obvious. On many occasions, anyone who is doing right will be persecuted or verbally tormented. Those bent on evil deeds like no alter-nate competition! So separation of these two Beatitudes is valid.

Notice that Jesus spoke specifically about verbal abuses (these would exclude physical torments). The eighth Beatitude is a generalized term that could include physical violence. The ninth Beatitude deals with verbal violence. We know that out of the mouth "come blessing and cursing" (James 3:10). We have been the recipients of both. Jesus proclaimed: "Out of the abundance of the heart the mouth speaks. . . . The evil man out of his evil treasure brings forth evil" (Matthew 12:34, 35).

And it doesn't take much contact with modern men to comprehend the depth of evil from which they speak. Language seems to have gained a new intensity in its abusive potential. Verbal blasts by evil men attack the very nature of their fellows and often leave no area of life unmolested. Such is the evil potential from the inner lives of evil people.

Notice the words Jesus uses: revile, persecute, utter all kinds of evil against you falsely—"on my account."

If we are persecuted because of some offbeat ideas we develop concerning religious beliefs or practices, it is not to our credit. We have no reason to become religiously obnoxious. In our witness we must always be gentle, kind, and considerate; not simply demanding that our words be totally accepted.

Many people listen regardless of the bizarre twists we give our religious presentations. Some Christians are verbally abused because they do not know when to stop witnessing. They have convinced themselves it is more important to get the witness out than to sense the response of the hearer and speak according to his need. Thus, they open themselves up to considerable verbal attack. Jesus didn't have these types of Christians, who don't really listen to the promptings of the Holy Spirit, in mind when He uttered this Beatitude.

But for that gentle, Holy Spirit controlled and prompted person who becomes the victim of evil men's revilings, accusings, and verbal blasts, Jesus had the utmost sympathy. Such a person, following in the pattern and standard of the witness developed by the Master himself, would be attacked even as Jesus was attacked.

Jesus said, "On my account." The Christian is persecuted because he is a representative of the divine Lord and is following His plan for living by eternal truths; his life-style does not mesh with that of people who seem bent on satisfying their continual hunger for pleasures. The real attack, according to Jesus, is not on the person but on the Christ within. The persecutor is opposing God, resisting the inroads of Jesus Christ, and bucking the eternal. Yet this is done not to the unseen Christ, but to the believer in Christ, because flesh-and-blood evil men pay no attention to the unseen.

Paul was acutely aware of this persecution of Jesus manifest through the evil attacks on his own person. He felt it a privilege to be so abused for Jesus' sake, although he did not seek such abuse. To the Christians at Philippi he said: "For it has been granted to you that for the sake of Christ you should not only believe in him but also suffer for his sake" (Philippians 1:29). He told them to engage "in the same conflict which you saw and now hear to be mine" (v. 30).

Evil men cannot attack Christ directly, so they attack those who believe and follow Him. Thus, we are exposed to persecution "on his account."

During our childhood, when other children taunted us or called us names, we sardonically replied, "Sticks and stones can break my bones, but names will never hurt me." All the while we knew we were uttering one of the world's biggest lies. Name-calling can do no bodily harm, that's true. But we also have a psyche. Psychologically, name-calling can be extremely painful.

Persecutors are well aware of the psychological pain they can inflict. Thus, coupled with any physical abuse, language abuse further penetrates the mind and psyche to tear down one's personality and integrity. Verbal attacks are often far more devastating to a person than physical deprivations. To break the body without breaking the soul eventually has little effect on the person. It is only a minor victory for the persecutor. Breaking the mind and soul eventually results in physical deterioration.

Jesus said men will "revile" His followers. They will assail the Christian with words that attack his integrity and degrade his character.

Didn't they do this to the Saviour? Didn't His opponents tear down His character? They called Him the son of Beelzebub and equated Him with the sinners He sought to upbuild. And the ultimate of their reviling came as He hung on the cross! Can we expect evil men to do less to the followers of the crucified Galilean?

Jesus said men will "utter all kinds of evil against you falsely." How like those who seek to tear down others to build themselves up. When they can't find a way to truthfully lower you, they resort to saying anything evil. They may start with a small immorally tainted story or a rumor—"Did you hear. . . ?" If possible, they twist associations, such as when they see you talking to a member of the opposite sex in front of one of the stores in town. They invent a "you-are-sexually-interested" story about you.

How easy for evil people to "utter all kinds of evil against you." It takes little or no intellectual or moral capacities to twist honest information into immoral or harmful gossip. Evil people delight in this. And in the process they become elated over your possible injury or demise.

Even though such reviling and evil talk hurts your reputation, take comfort in the fact that it is falsely spoken. Although you may have to spend considerable time clearing your name because of such false information and character assassination, remember that evil men have always practiced such. They have done it to the best of men. They did it to Christ.

A natural man would react in anger to these unjustified attacks. He would fight back with equally abusive, or at least equally pungent, words. He would defend his reputation. But Jesus told His followers to take a different approach; to use a different tactic—possibly to preserve personal sanity, but also to counterattack the attacker. Who can tear down one who doesn't defend himself? Who can further hurt one who doesn't bristle when attacked? Who can more deeply abuse one who shows no outward signs of being abused?

Jesus said His followers should not react like natural men but do just the opposite: "Rejoice and be glad." (Maybe not in the presence of the persecutor, but sometime after being persecuted.) How contrary to the general reaction to adversity! Adversity usually causes bitterness or at least complaint. But Jesus says, "Rejoice!"

What did He know that we usually don't? He knew what Paul later stated in Romans 5:3-5: "We rejoice in our sufferings, knowing that suffering produces endurance, and endurance produces character, and character produces hope, and hope does not disappoint us, because God's love has been poured into our hearts through the Holy Spirit which has been given to us."

85

Rejoice, because persecution, even though it is most painful at the time of infliction, produces Christian character and makes us more into the likeness of Jesus Christ.

What does Christ promise us if we follow this Beatitude? A future reward! Not an entrance into the kingdom of heaven; that has already been promised for following previous Beatitudes. Christ tells us we will have our reward in heaven; something special; something eternal.

If you are persecuted because of your affiliation with Jesus Christ, count it all joy. The reward that will be yours forever is worth the reviling, evil speaking, and false reporting about your transformed character. Count it all joy. Your reward will come!

11

Finding a Reason
for Existence

To sum up the Beatitudes, let us again say that
Jesus did not give these to us to condemn us, but to
give us goals to strive for. If you are a long way from
realizing what He said, you must not let these words
whip you into despair. Rather, let them lift you into
the possibility of what you can be. Both the first and
the last Beatitude end with the promise of the kingdom of heaven. That's what God really has for you!

The story of the American railroads is one that can
benefit us all. The railroads incorrectly diagnosed
their purpose. At the turn of the century, the railroad
men were the "big boys," and they let everyone
know about their superiority.

Then one day an entrepreneur got the idea that he
could make some money by picking up and delivering railway freight that normally was just shoved out
of the railroad car onto the loading dock 3 feet below.
This fellow developed a profitable business and in a
few years had "bitten off a leg" of the railroad industry. Another businessman started delivering cargo
by trucks from city to city and state to state. Pretty
soon, the trucking business had bitten off another leg

ιe railroads. Then a third man found a way to ansport people without submitting to the delays, overbearing attitudes, and rules of the railroads. And the bus lines bit an arm off the railroads.

Finally, some people thought of a way to move goods and passengers by air. In its early stages, all the airlines in America could have been purchased out of the petty cash funds of the railroad industry. But the airlines came along and bit off another arm of the railroad business.

What is the moral of this story? The railroads missed their reason for being. They were in the railroad business rather than the transportation industry.

What is the application of this to the Beatitudes? If you go through life with your own narrow goals, you will not only miss the reason for your existence, but someone else will get all that God desires you to get from life. Strive for the goals of Christ, what He wants you to have, and your life will be blessed of God and beneficial to others! Such a life is truly the "blessed" life!